THE WORLD OF SCIENCE

THE WORLD TODAY

THE WORLD OF SCIENCE

THE WORLD TODAY

KEITH LYE

Facts On File Publications
New York, New York • Bicester, England

First published in the United States of America in 1986
by Facts on File, Inc., 460 Park Avenue South, New
York, N.Y. 10016

First published in Great Britain in 1986 by Orbis
Publishing Limited, London

Library of Congress Cataloging in Publication Data

Main entry under title:
World of Science

   Includes index.
   Summary: A twenty-five volume encyclopedia of
scientific subjects, designed for eight- to twelve-year-
olds. One volume is entirely devoted to projects.
   1. Science—Dictionaries, Juvenile.   1. Science—
Dictionaries
Q121.J86 1984   500   84-1654

ISBN: 0-8160- 1072-2

Printed in Italy
10 9 8 7 6 5 4 3 2 1

Consultant editors
Eleanor Felder, Former Managing Editor, *New Book of
Knowledge*
James Neujahr, Dean of the School of Education, City
College of New York
Ethan Signer, Professor of Biology, Massachusetts
Institute of Technology
J. Tuzo Wilson, Director General, Ontario Science
Centre

Previous pages
The world today is a
tremendous mixture.
This Black girl is an
American, but her
ancestors came from
West Africa. Her home
is in New Orleans,
which the French, the
first European settlers
in the area, named
after France's second
city.

Editor Penny Clarke
Designer Roger Kohn

CONTENTS

Note There are some unusual words in this book. They are explained in the Glossary on pages 62–63. The first time each word is used it is printed in *italics*.

▼The Zulus are one of the principal tribes of southern Africa. Traditionally, they were great warriors and are renowned for their bravery.

HUMAN HISTORY

In barely 50,000 years, the human family has conquered the Earth. Unlike any other creatures in the Earth's history, humans have changed the land on which they live. And with their great intelligence and use of language, they have founded many complex religions and social systems.

HUMAN ORIGINS

Scientists place people in the highest order (group) of mammals, the *primates*. This order also includes apes, monkeys, tree shrews and lemurs. The *fossils* of early primates, which resembled tree shrews, have been found in rocks dating back 60 million years.

Fossils of the ancestors of modern apes date back more than 30 million years. Human ancestry is more mysterious. Some scientists have suggested that our ancestor might have been a human-like ape, which they call *Ramapithecus*, which lived between about 14 and 9 million years ago. No one knows for sure, because practically no fossils of human-like creatures have been found in rocks formed between 9 and 4 million years ago.

About 4 million years ago, a human-like creature called *Australopithecus* (a word meaning 'southern ape') appeared. This creature walked upright and scientists once thought that it was the 'link' between *Ramapithecus* and the human family. But fossils have recently been found of other, more advanced creatures, who lived alongside *Australopithecus*. One called *Homo*

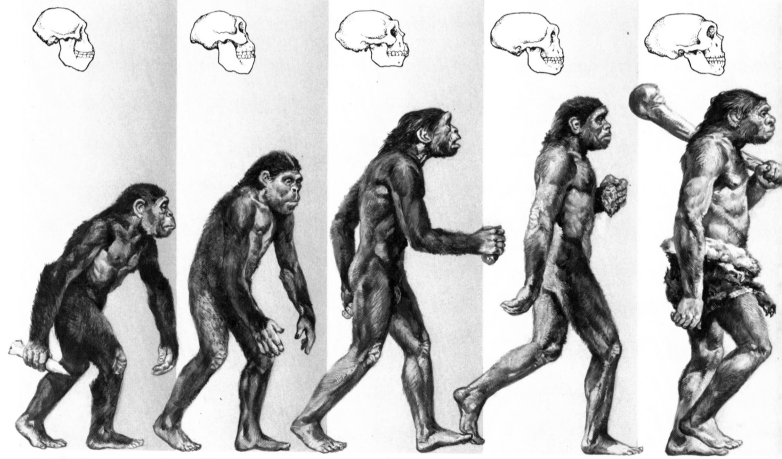

Australopithecus   *Homo habilis*   *Homo erectus*   *Homo sapiens*   Neanderthal Man

▲Many fossils of early man-like creatures have been found in the East African Rift Valley. Some experts regard this region as the cradle of the human family.

Cro-Magnon Man

◄Human evolution is still not fully understood. But scientists have studied fossils of various ape-like creatures which resemble people in certain ways. One such creature called *Australopithecus* lived from about 4 million to perhaps 500,000 years ago. It walked upright, hunted and gathered plant food. But it was not one of our ancestors, because there were more advanced man-like creatures living at the same time. For example, *Homo erectus* first appeared about 1.6 million years ago. It had a larger brain than *Australopithecus*, but it had several ape-like features, such as a flattened face and flattened front to the skull. Cro-Magnon Man, whose fossils were found in south-western France, lived about 35,000 years ago. This early man belongs to our species (*Homo sapiens sapiens*).

habilis ('handy man') was a tool-maker, and fossils for this creature date back 1.75 million years. And about 1.6 million years ago, *Homo erectus* ('upright man') appeared. Its fossils have been found in many places, including Africa, China (where it is called Peking Man), and in Indonesia (Java Man). *Homo erectus* became *extinct* about 300,000 years ago.

The earliest type of modern people, *Homo sapiens* ('intelligent man') probably appeared first about 500,000 years ago. The fossils of one type were called Neanderthal Man, because they were found in the Neander valley in Germany.

7

▲Early people led a nomadic (wandering) life. Once farming had begun many people chose a settled life. Some remained hunters and gatherers. Others bred animals and moved around in search of pasture or from oasis to oasis, like these Berbers in Morocco.

▶The early development of religion was linked with magic. Magic and witchcraft still occur in some societies. Some people believe this South African witch doctor has the power to cure the sick and cast magic spells.

Neanderthal Man, known to scientists as *Homo sapiens neanderthalensis*, lived between about 100,000 and 10,000 years ago. Modern people, called *Homo sapiens sapiens* (to distinguish us from Neanderthal Man) emerged around 50,000 years ago.

Early societies

For most of human history, people lived by hunting animals and gathering plants and roots for food. We get some idea of how they lived by studying hunting and gathering societies which still exist. These include the pygmies and Bushmen in Africa and the Aborigines of Australia.

Hunting and gathering people led nomadic (wandering) lives, mostly in small groups. Because they were always on the move, they had few possessions. But they were successful and seldom starved, because they knew about animal *migrations* and the seasonal growth of plants. They developed religions, possibly to bring them success when they were hunting. Many *prehistoric* cave paintings show hunters and their prey. Such paintings may have been connected with magic and religious rites. But the hunter-gatherers had little need for *government*. Ideas of government arose when more complicated societies were founded.

The beginning of farming

About 10,000 years ago, the *Ice Age* had ended and it was much warmer throughout the world. In these favourable conditions, the human family took a great step forward. This was the invention of farming. It took place first in south-western Asia and, soon afterwards, in other parts of the world. Many hunter-gatherers became settled farmers. *Agriculture* gave them much more control over their food supply.

Extra food led to an increase in population and the creation of villages and towns. The oldest known walled town was Jericho (now El Ariha), north-east of modern Jerusalem. In about 7800 BC, some 3,000 people lived in Jericho. In towns, people worked at jobs other than farming. Their tools were made of stone and bone. But gradually metals came into use. By 4000 BC, copper objects were common in south-western Asia. By around 3000 BC, bronze, an alloy (mixture) of copper and tin, had largely replaced the softer copper.

The rise of modern civilization
The development of *technology* made the rise of early civilizations possible. Major civilizations sprang up in river valleys, notably those of the Tigris and Euphrates rivers (in what is now Iraq), the Nile (Egypt), and the Indus (Pakistan). The rivers were used to irrigate (water) the land in the valleys. Farmers no longer had to rely on rainfall. New crops were developed and new kinds of domestic animals were bred. Plant and animal *breeding* continue to this day.

The Iron Age began in south-western Asia in about 1200 BC. The widespread introduction of iron, a harder metal than bronze, marked the start of modern times. The Iron Age continued until the *Industrial Revolution* began in the late eighteenth century.

The Industrial Revolution caused other changes in human society. Most important, it led to the growth of huge industrial cities. But other types of societies, including those of hunter-gatherers, nomadic pastoralists (livestock herders), and subsistence farmers who produce only enough food for their families, still exist alongside advanced industrial societies.

▲Ancient and modern methods of harvesting grain. **Top** An ancient Egyptian tomb painting shows a farmer cutting the grain with a sickle and a woman picking it up. **Above** Machines now cut, pick up and separate the grain from the straw in one operation.

►This riverside industrial area is in the United States. The Industrial Revolution began in Britain in the late 18th century. It has brought many changes to the ways of life of people in industrial nations.

THE HUMAN FAMILY

The human family is often divided into four main sub-groups: Caucasoid, Mongoloid, Negroid and Australoid. These sub-groups are often called 'races'. But the term 'race' has often been wrongly used. For example, the Nazis in Germany in World War 2 said that the Jews were an inferior race. This idea of race is incorrect. Most Jews belong to exactly the same sub-group or 'race' as the Germans. Both are Caucasoids. There are differences between Jews and Germans, but these are *cultural* and religious differences, not racial ones.

Caucasoids include most Europeans and people of European descent who live in other continents. Darker-skinned people of western Asia and most North Africans, including Arabs and Berbers, are also Caucasoids.

The Mongoloid sub-group includes most people in eastern Asia and the Eskimos and Indians of North and South America. People of this sub-group have yellow skins and straight dark hair.

The Negroid sub-group includes the Black people of Africa and the descendants of African slaves taken to the Americas. The pygmies of central Africa and the Khoisan group (Bushmen and Hottentots) of southern Africa resemble Negroids. But they are sufficiently different for some *anthropologists* to regard them as separate. Another people, called Negritos, live in south-eastern Asia. They resemble Blacks but are smaller, so they, too, are often regarded as separate.

The Australoids include the Australian Aborigines. These people are sometimes called 'Archaic Whites'. They are descendants of an ancient people who were probably common in Asia before the Caucasoids and Mongoloids had emerged as separate sub-groups. Similar people include the Veddoids of southern India and Sri Lanka (Ceylon), and the Ainu, the first inhabitants of Japan. Some Polynesians who live on Pacific islands are also of mixed ancestry.

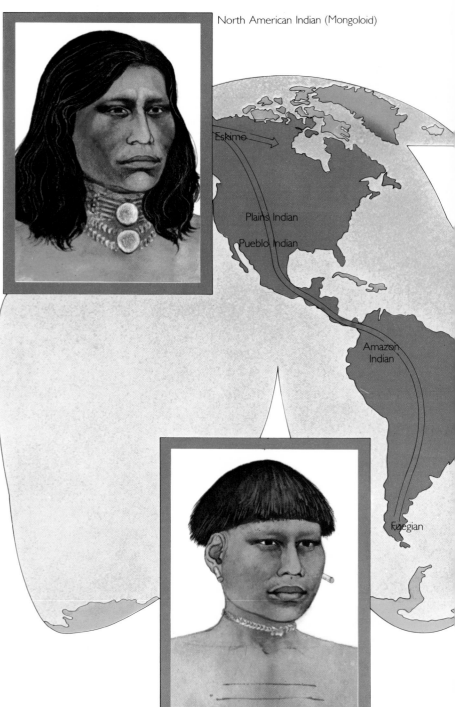

North American Indian (Mongoloid)

Eskimo

Plains Indian

Pueblo Indian

Amazon Indian

Fuegian

South American Indian (Mongoloid)

Human migrations have led to much mixing of the sub-groups. This mixing is continuing today, especially because travel has become easier and cheaper. Some countries welcome immigrants. For example, the United States has been called a 'melting pot' of peoples, who have come from all parts of the world.

Arab (Caucasoid)

Japanese (Mongoloid)

African (Negroid)

Australian Aborigine (Australoid)

▲The human family is divided into four main sub-groups. The Caucasoids include most Europeans and most people in western Asia and northern Africa. Most Mongoloids live in eastern Asia. The Eskimos and the American Indians are also Mongoloids. Negroid people live in southern and central Africa. This group also includes the Black communities in the Americas. The Australoids include the Australian Aborigines.

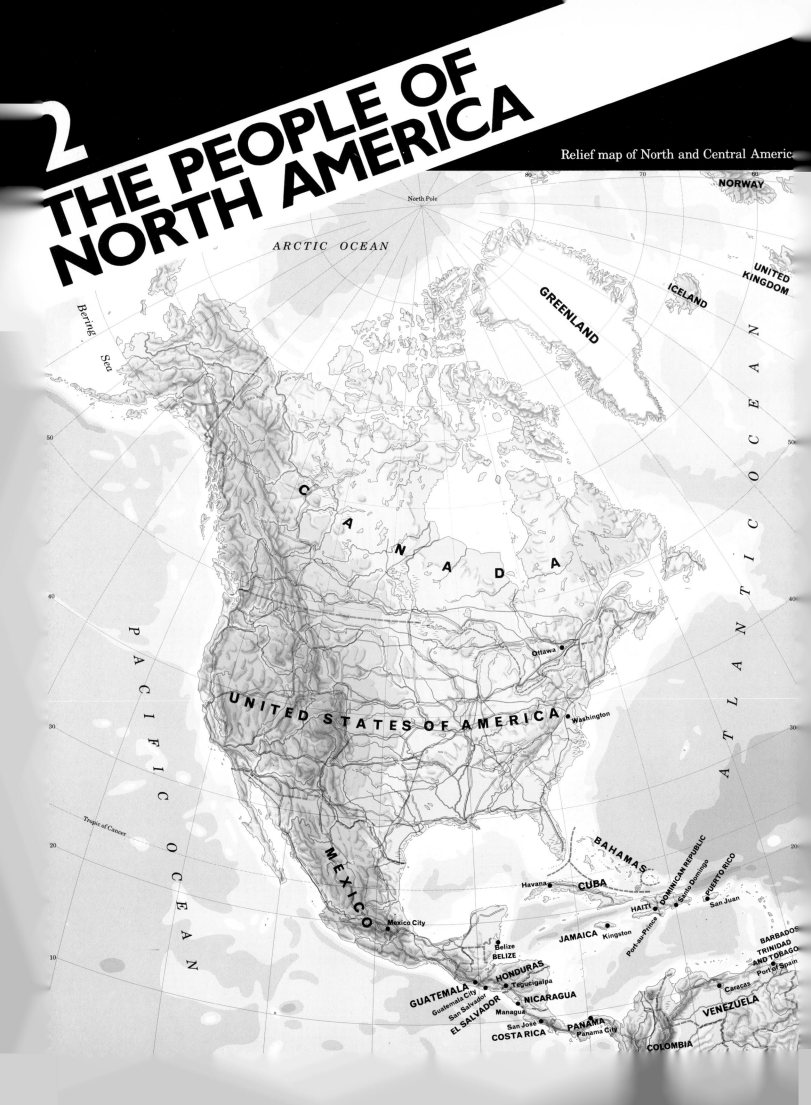

Relief map of North and Central America

The first Americans settled in the continent in the Ice Age, which ended 10,000 years ago. The sea-level was much lower than it is now. This was because so much of the world's water was frozen in thick ice sheets. As a result, the Bering Strait, which now separates Alaska from the USSR, was dry land. Across this land bridge came the Mongoloid ancestors of the American Indians (or Amerindians). No one knows exactly when this occurred. Some *archaeologists* think that it was about 40,000 years ago.

The Eskimos probably reached North America about 12,000 years ago. They spread across Canada and Greenland. Farming was impossible in the polar lands, but the Eskimos were skilful hunters and fine craftsmen.

◄A North American Indian wearing a ceremonial headdress.

▶A Mexican Indian woman weaving a basket. An intricately patterned finished basket stands beside her.

NORTH AMERICAN INDIANS

Nine major American Indian nations lived in Canada and the United States. Each nation contained several subdivisions using different languages. Their lifestyles differed. The northern Subarctic Indians consisted mostly of hunters and fishermen. They had no permanent villages. By contrast, the North-West Coast Indians could get food, especially fish, more easily. They lived settled lives and their artists were famous for their wood carvings.

The North-East Woodland Indians were farmers or hunters. They include the Iroquois, who built large farming villages. The Iroquois developed ideas of government. They banded together in *confederacies* (alliances) to help each other. The South-Eastern Indians, including the Cherokee, Choctaw, Creek and Seminole, also lived settled lives, generally in prosperous farming villages.

The Plains Indians were farmers and hunters. Their brilliant method of fighting on horseback, shown in many Western movies, was not possible until Spanish explorers brought horses to North America. Horses were formerly unknown, but the Plains Indians rapidly became superb riders and hunters of

buffalo (American bison).

In the western mountains, the Plateau Indians of the north-west built villages. Some farmed but others lived mainly by hunting and gathering, like the Great Basin Indians to the south. By contrast, the Indians of western California occupied much richer land and had more complex societies. The South-Western Indians included the Pueblo, who are known for their impressive stone and *adobe* homes, often several storeys high.

More advanced societies grew up in Mexico and Central America, including those of the *Maya* and *Toltec*. The *Aztecs* founded a powerful empire in central Mexico in about AD 1200.

▲The faces of these Eskimos have similarities to the faces of the North American Indian (**top**) and Mexican Indian (**above**). This suggests that their distant ancestors came from the same region, probably north-east Asia, before migrating to North America.

The arrival of Europeans
The explorer Christopher Columbus discovered the West Indies in 1492. He thought, wrongly, that he had reached Asia and so he called the local people Indians. Columbus claimed the area for Spain. Spanish soldiers soon overran Mexico and Central America, destroying the Indian civilizations.

▼The map shows that people from many parts of the world have settled in North America. Apart from the American Indians and Eskimos, the immigrants all arrived in the last 500 years.

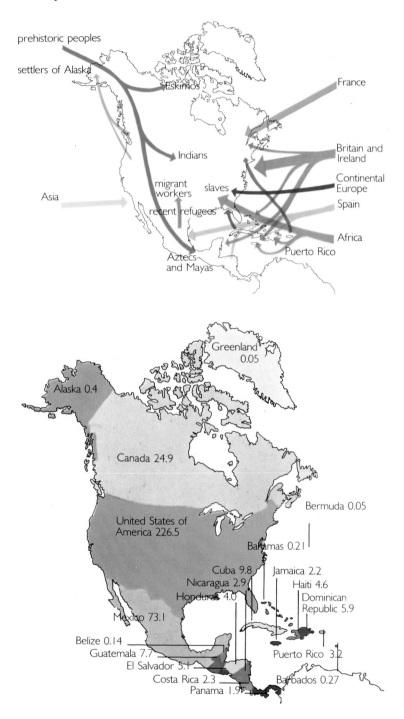

▲The map shows the chief countries of North America and Central America. The figures are the populations of the countries in millions.

The mixing of Spanish and Indian cultures produced a Latin American culture. Latin American countries have official languages (Spanish, Portuguese or French) which are based on Latin, the language of ancient Rome. These languages are called Romance languages. The mixing of peoples was complicated by the introduction of African slaves. Mixing led to the creation of two new groups. The *mestizos* are people of mixed Indian and European origin. The *mulattos* are of mixed African and European descent.

The British and French opened up Canada and the United States. They built settlements and founded colonies. At first European countries controlled North America. But, one by one, the North American countries chose to rule themselves. Each created distinctive cultures, blending European and local influences. Today, only a few West Indian island territories are still ruled by European nations.

CANADA

Canada, the world's second largest country after the USSR, is thinly populated. The north is too cold for farming and most people live in the south, near the border with the United States. Canada is a rich country and its people enjoy a high standard of living.

Canada had 24,343,000 people in 1981. The American Indians and Inuit (Eskimos) now make up only 1.6 per cent of the population. Many Indians and Inuit have adopted western ways of life. Most Canadians are of European origin, especially British or French. But there are sizeable groups from other parts of Europe.

English and French are the official languages. In the 1981 *census*, 61.3 per cent of the people said that English was their mother tongue and 25.7 per cent French. French-speaking Canadians are concentrated in the province of Quebec. They are proud of their French culture. Some want to make Quebec a separate country. But a majority of the people of Quebec voted in 1981 to stay part of Canada.

THE UNITED STATES

The United States is the world's most industrialized country and one of the two great superpowers. It is the world's fourth largest country, both in area and population. It consists of 50 states, 48 of which lie between Canada and Mexico. The other states are Alaska in the cold north-west corner of North America, and the tropical islands of Hawaii in the central Pacific Ocean.

The country has enormous natural resources, including fertile farmland and large reserves of most minerals. But manufacturing is the most important economic activity. About 79 per cent of the people live in cities and towns.

In the 1980 census, the United States had more than 226 million people. Of these, 83.1 per cent are White (Caucasoids) and 11.7 per cent are Blacks. Most Blacks are the descendants of slaves. There are also groups of American Indians, Chinese, Filipinos, Japanese, Mexican, Puerto Rican, Polynesian (Hawaiian) and other peoples.

When Europeans began to settle in North America, the American Indians probably numbered about 2,000,000. But numbers fell because of wars and *epidemics* of diseases to which the Indians had no resistance. By 1900, only 237,000 Indians were left. By 1980, the Indian

▼Photographed from Skylab, Chicago looks more like a small town than a huge sprawling industrial city.

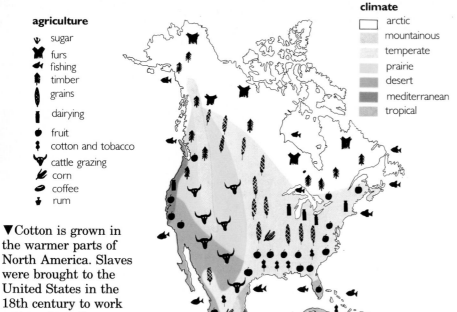

agriculture

- ⚘ sugar
- 🦫 furs
- 🐟 fishing
- 🌲 timber
- ⫮ grains
- ⫯ dairying
- 🍒 fruit
- ⫯ cotton and tobacco
- ⊻ cattle grazing
- 🌿 corn
- ☕ coffee
- ⫯ rum

climate

- ☐ arctic
- mountainous
- temperate
- prairie
- desert
- mediterranean
- tropical

◀The map shows the various climatic regions of North America, ranging from the icy Arctic to tropical Central America. Farm products vary according to the climate.

▼Cotton is grown in the warmer parts of North America. Slaves were brought to the United States in the 18th century to work cotton plantations. Slavery was ended by the American Civil War (1861–63). Today, cotton is gathered by machines.

population had grown again to 1,420,000. But this represents less than one per cent of the total population.

The United States is proud of being a 'land of opportunity'. Its economy is based on free enterprise. Many people enjoy a high standard of living, but some groups, such as some Blacks, Mexicans and American Indians, are poor. In theory, anyone can become the president or a millionaire, if they work hard. Because everyone has the chance of moving upwards, American society is said to be 'socially mobile'.

Society is also mobile, because people often move home to get better jobs. As a result, most American families are nuclear. This means that families consist only of parents and their children, while other relations, such as grandparents, aunts and uncles, often live a long distance away. Nuclear families are the opposite of extended families. In extended families, parents and their children live close to their other relations. Extended families are uncommon in the United States.

▶Nearly four-fifths of the people of the United States live in cities and towns. The country contains many large cities, such as Chicago, Illinois, shown here at night.

▶Several American cities, including San Francisco, California, have a district called Chinatown (**inset**). In 1980, the United States had more than 800,000 citizens of Chinese origin.

MEXICO AND CENTRAL AMERICA

Mexico is North America's third largest country. Its people are much poorer than those of Canada and the USA. Many of the people are peasant farmers and manufacturing is not very important. But Mexico is developing quickly.

There are seven Central American countries. In order of size, they are Nicaragua, Honduras, Guatemala, Panama, Costa Rica, Belize and El Salvador. Spanish is the official language in all of them except Belize. Belize was formerly called British Honduras. It became independent in 1981 and English is its official language.

Throughout Central America, the main religion is Roman Catholicism. But many pre-Spanish beliefs are evident in religious festivals. For example, the Aztecs were fascinated by death. Skulls and skeletons are common in their paintings. Their fascination is recalled on All Souls Day (called the Day of the Dead in Mexico). Some people wear costumes with skeletons painted on them, and sugar skulls and skulls painted on bread are also part of the traditions surrounding this day.

Mestizos form a major group in Mexico and Central America, although there are large American Indian groups, especially in Mexico, Guatemala and Belize. There are also people of Black African and European origin. Apart from Costa Rica and Panama, the people live, on average, at least 10 years less than Canadian and US citizens. Living standards are lower and medical and educational services fewer.

▼Colourful markets can be seen throughout Mexico. Mexican culture is a blend of American Indian and Spanish traditions. Spanish is the official language, although many Indian languages are also spoken.

THE WEST INDIES

The people of the West Indies are also a complex mix of various peoples. Only a few, and they are now of mixed origin, are descended from the original population. Most people today are descendants of Europeans, Africans and, in some places, Asians who were originally brought to the islands as labourers after slavery had been abolished.

The largest countries are Cuba and the Dominican Republic. Spanish is their official language and so they are considered part of Latin America. This is also true of the third largest nation, Haiti, where French is the official tongue. But some nations, such as the Bahamas, Jamaica and Trinidad and Tobago, have English as their official language, and so they are not regarded as part of Latin America. Puerto Rico, a Commonwealth of the USA, has two official languages:

Spanish and English. Some islands are still ruled by European countries, namely Britain (Antigua), France (Montserrat) and the Netherlands (the Antilles). Farming, fishing and tourism are the main activities in the West Indies. Many people are poor, but West Indian culture is marked by high spirits, which are expressed in exciting carnivals.

▲Preparing a steel band for a carnival in Trinidad and Tobago. Blacks form the leading community in this Caribbean country. Drumming was introduced by the Blacks from Africa.

◄An impromptu music session gets under way on the beach in Puerto Rico in the West Indies. Most people are of Black African and European descent.

3 THE PEOPLE OF SOUTH AMERICA

American Indians crossed the narrow land bridge (now Panama) some 20,000 years ago. They spread south throughout South America, the world's fourth largest continent. They probably reached the southern tip of South America about 11,000 years ago.

By the time that Christopher Columbus reached the West Indies, South America probably had more than 10 million American Indians. More than half lived in the Inca empire.

THE INCA EMPIRE

The Inca empire was founded in the high Andes mountains of Peru. By about AD 1500, its power extended into what is now Ecuador, Bolivia and Chile.

The empire was controlled by an army that moved around along an excellent network of roads. The Incas did not use the wheel, instead they used pack animals to carry goods over the steep, mountainous land. But the Incas were great engineers. They built huge stone cities and step-like terraces down hillsides. They grew crops on these terraces, using *irrigation channels* to water the fields.

The Incas had complicated social, political and military systems and their artists made beautiful pottery and metal objects. Their advanced way of life contrasted with that of other South American Indian groups. The Indians in the north, near the Caribbean Sea, were farmers and hunters. Some Indians who lived in the vast rain forests ('selvas') of the Amazon river basin were hunter-gatherers. Others farmed. They cleared a

◄The Incas built up a powerful American Indian empire in Peru. Ruins of its cities prove that the people were fine engineers and builders. The empire was founded between AD 1100 and 1200. In the 1530s, Spanish forces conquered most of Peru and seized the Incas' treasures. They forced many people into slavery.

USA

CUBA

DOMINICAN
REPUBLIC

PUERTO RICO

HAITI

JAMAICA

BELIZE

MEXICO

HONDURAS

BARBADOS

GUATEMALA

NICARAGUA

TRINIDAD AND
TOBAGO

EL SALVADOR

Caracas

COSTA RICA

PANAMA

VENEZUELA

GUYANA

Georgetown

Paramaribo

Bogotá

SURINAM

Cayenne

COLOMBIA

FRENCH
GUIANA

Quito

Equator

ECUADOR

P
A
C
I
F
I
C

O
C
E
A
N

BRAZIL

P
E
R
U

Lima

BOLIVIA

Brasília

La Paz

A
T
L
A
N
T
I
C

O
C
E
A
N

PARAGUAY

Tropic of Capricorn

Asuncion

C
H
I
L
E

A
R
G
E
N
T
I
N
A

URUGUAY

Santiago

Buenos Aires

Montevideo

0   500   1000   1500

km

patch of forest and planted crops. After a few years, when the soil was less fertile, they moved to a new patch. The old farm was soon overgrown. This method, called shifting cultivation or slash and burn, is still used today. Other groups of Indians lived on the grasslands of southern South America. Most were wandering hunters-and-gatherers.

European rule

Spanish soldiers destroyed the Inca empire in the 1530s, making many people slaves. Spain soon ruled most of South America. Portugal took Brazil and the Roman Catholic Church became the leading church in the continent. A Latin American culture, like that of Central America, soon evolved. However, in the seventeenth century, British, Dutch and French settlers moved into areas in the north-east.

When South Americans heard that the United States had declared its independence of Britain in 1776, they, too, wanted freedom. In the early nineteenth century, the Spanish-ruled countries and Brazil won their independence. The small British, Dutch and French territories, however, had to wait for political advances. British Guiana became independent in 1966 as Guyana. Dutch Guiana became independent as Surinam in 1975. French Guiana, an overseas 'département' of France, is still ruled as part of France.

SOUTH AMERICA TODAY

The South American mainland is divided into 13 countries. Spanish is the official language in nine of them: Colombia (population 29 million), Argentina (28 million), Peru (20 million), Venezuela (16 million), Chile (12 million), Ecuador (9.6 million), Bolivia (6.5 million), Paraguay (3.6 million) and Uruguay (3 million).

Portuguese is Brazil's official language. Brazil, South America's biggest and the world's fifth largest country, is South America's giant, in both area and population—130 million people in 1983.

English is the official language in Guyana (population 903,000), Dutch in Surinam (415,000) and French in French Guiana (73,000).

Many American Indian languages are still spoken. Countries with large American Indian populations are Peru, Ecuador and Bolivia, the land of the Incas. The cultures of these three countries are now, in fact, more Indian than Spanish. Some countries have small Indian populations, but large numbers of mestizos, as in Colombia and Venezuela in the north, and Paraguay and Chile in the south. Blacks and mulattos, the descendants of African slaves, form major groups in Colombia, Venezuela, Brazil, Guyana, Surinam and French Guiana. Guyana and Surinam also have large communities of Asian descent. People of European origin form the majority in Argentina, Brazil and Uruguay.

◀Bolivia is one of the most under-developed countries in South America. Much of the land is so poor that the farmers can grow little more than enough to feed their families. Anything extra is sold at a local market, but it is seldom enough to pay for more modern equipment.

►The population map shows that much of the interior of South America is thinly populated. The chief centres of population are along the coasts or on tropical plateaus (tablelands), which are cooler than the lowlands.

people per square mile

	uninhabited
	less than 2
	2–25
	25–50
	50–250
	more than 250

▲The map shows some of South America's many natural resources, together with the main cattle, pig and sheep-rearing regions. Argentina and Brazil are developing quickly. They are both on the way to becoming great industrial powers.

South American societies

By comparison with northern North America and Europe, South America is a poor, *developing* continent. The wealthiest country is Venezuela, the world's seventh largest oil producer. Brazil and Argentina have enormous resources, which are only partly developed. Experts think that Brazil and Argentina will become leading industrial nations in 40 to 50 years time.

The poorest country is Bolivia. Bolivians live, on average, 51 years, as compared with 64 to 70 years in most of South America. Bolivia has also the worst educational record. Only 63 per cent of adults can read and write, as compared with 93 per cent in Argentina and 74 per cent in Brazil.

South America contains one of the world's most complicated mixtures of peoples. There is little racial discrimination (pages 10–11). But there are often great differences between the rich few and the poor. The rich are often of European origin.

In some countries, the mestizos form a middle group between the rich Europeans and the poor. This is particularly marked in Peru and Bolivia, where mestizos, called Chollos, dominate commercial life. In southern South America, people of European origin dominate society. For example, the Argentinian Indians were either killed or died of European diseases. They now form only 2 per cent of the population. A group of Spanish families became great land-owners. They ran the country and introduced a form of behaviour called 'machismo'. This means that men see themselves as the protectors of their families. They dominate their families, especially the women who are made to feel inferior. This contrasts with such countries as Chile where women play a major role in society.

South America is a fast-changing continent, with a rapidly increasing population. In places, cities are growing so quickly that many people are forced to live in unhealthy slums around the outskirts. The way of life of the unemployed in the slums contrasts with

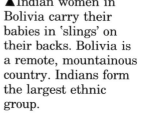

▶There are
tremendous extremes
of wealth and poverty
in South America.
These Indians from
Guayaquil, Ecuador's
chief port, have taken
their dug-out canoes
alongside a big cargo
vessel to beg for food.

▲Indian women in
Bolivia carry their
babies in 'slings' on
their backs. Bolivia is
a remote, mountainous
country. Indians form
the largest ethnic
group.

that of the rich people who work in the city skyscrapers.

The drift of people to the cities is marked in Brazil, where the population is increasing by just over 2 per cent (about 2.73 million) a year. Brazilians are rapidly developing their huge country. They are now building roads into the Amazon forests. They are clearing the trees to make way for farms, towns, dams and mines. This development is good for Brazil as a whole. But contact with outsiders is destroying the Indians. Many have been ill-treated by the newcomers, while others have died of common European diseases, such as 'flu, to which the Indians have no resistance. Some Indians are now protected in special reservations, such as the Xingu National Park, but their numbers are still declining. Brazil now has only an estimated 200,000 Indians.

◀Men of the Yanomamo tribe of Indians that live in Amazon basin rainforests. The blow pipe is one of their chief weapons.

▼These two photographs vividly show the extremes in South American society. The spacious layout and expensive international design of the war memorial in Rio de Janeiro, Brazil, is in sharp contrast to the shanty town slum (**inset**) in the centre of the same city.

4 THE PEOPLE OF EUROPE AND THE USSR

Europe is the smallest continent apart from Oceania (page 48). It contains 32 independent nations, together with 25 per cent of the USSR and 3 per cent of Turkey.

►Relief map of Europe, Turkey and western and central Russia.

EUROPEAN CIVILIZATION

European, or western, civilization has its roots in ancient Greece and Rome. The Romans spread Christianity, a major element in western civilization, through much of Europe. There are now three main Christian movements: the Orthodox Church in the USSR and south-eastern Europe; the Roman Catholic Church in the south; and Protestant Churches in the north and parts of the west.

From the fifteenth century, explorers and missionaries carried western ideas around the world. Great empires were founded and people of European origin became the majority in North America and Oceania. New skills were acquired in the Industrial Revolution. As a result, mining and manufacturing replaced farming as the main activity in most parts of Europe.

Today, Europe's overseas empires have disappeared and most former *colonies* are independent. But Europe remains a prosperous and mostly industrialized continent, although Europeans face various problems. For example, most countries have one or more minority language groups. Some of these groups would like to rule themselves. Europe is also divided politically into the West and the *Communist* East.

PEOPLE AND LANGUAGES

Most Europeans are Caucasoids. Their ancestors originally came from the Caucasus region in the USSR. Caucasoid people vary in appearance. For example, many Mediterranean people are of medium stature, with dark hair, brown eyes and light brown skin, while Nordic people (in Norway and Sweden) are tall, fair-haired and blue-eyed. East Baltic people, including many Finns, Poles and Russians, are similar to the Nordic type, except that they have heads that are broader in shape. Alpine people in south-central Europe also have those broad heads, but they are of medium height and thick-set. Because of inter-mixing, these groups are no longer distinct in many places.

Most European languages belong to the Indo-European language family. They all derive from one ancient language which has been lost. The Indo-European family is divided into several groups. Romance languages (French, Italian, Portuguese,

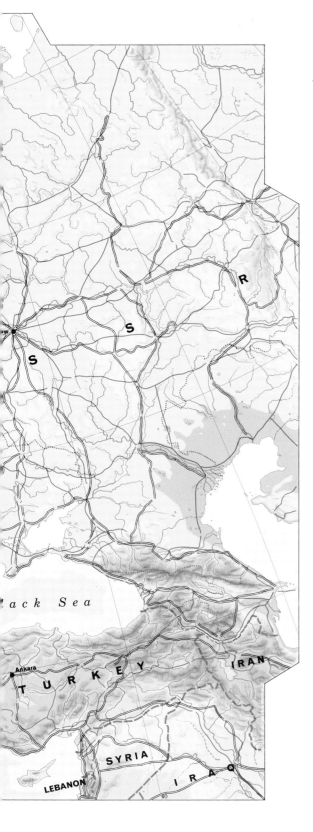

Romanian and Spanish) are derived from Latin. Germanic languages include English, Dutch and German. The Scandinavian languages include Icelandic, Norwegian and Swedish, and Balto-Slavic languages include Bulgarian, Czech, Polish, Russian, Slovak and Ukrainian. A few languages are not Indo-European. For example, Finnish and Hungarian belong to the Uralic and Altaic families (page 36).

NORTHERN EUROPE

Scandinavia

Scandinavia includes Sweden (population 8.3 million), Denmark (5.1 million), Finland (4.8 million), Norway (4.1 million) and Iceland (231,000). All except Denmark have cold climates and are thinly populated. But northern Europe is prosperous. The people enjoy high standards of living, with free welfare services for all. One minority group, the Lapps, live in northern Norway, Sweden, Finland and the USSR. The Lapps are nomads who follow the annual migrations of the reindeer. They eat reindeer meat, use reindeer as beasts of burden and make clothes and tents from reindeer skins. Some Lapps, particularly in Sweden, now live in settlements.

▲Dutch engineers have reclaimed land which was once under the sea. They do this by building walls, called dykes, to hold back the sea. The Dutch have saying: God created the world, but the Dutch made Holland.

▼Traditional costumes are worn at a wedding in Norway. Norway is a mostly Protestant country and the Evangelical Lutheran Church is the national church.

The Low Countries

The Low Countries include the Netherlands (population 14.2 million), Belgium (9.9 million) and Luxembourg (364,000). These countries are densely populated and prosperous. They became rich because of their efficient farming, their engineering skills in *land reclamation* and their highly organized industries. One country, Belgium, has two main groups of people. The Flemings in the north speak a form of Dutch, while the Walloons in the south speak French. Differences between these peoples have caused riots.

The Low Countries were founder members, with France, West Germany and Italy, of the European Economic Community, or EEC. The EEC aims at expanding the economies of its members. It was founded in 1957. In 1973, Britain, Ireland and Denmark joined the EEC. Greece followed in 1981.

The British Isles

The British Isles consists of the United Kingdom of Great Britain and Northern Ireland (population 56 million) and the Republic of Ireland (3.4 million).

The British have a strong sense of nationhood and pride in their historical traditions. They led the way in the Industrial Revolution and by the end of the nineteenth century ruled the world's largest empire. Britain is a densely populated industrial nation. But recently, other nations have overtaken Britain economically. In addition, Britain faced problems arising from unemployment, inflation and unrest in Northern Ireland. There, the Irish Republican Army (IRA) wants Northern Ireland to break from Britain and to be united with the Republic of Ireland. Most Northern Irelanders oppose this policy.

The Republic of Ireland, once linked with Britain, is now a separate country. Irish, a *Celtic language*, and English are spoken. Farming and processing farm products are the main industries.

France, Germany and Central Europe

France (population 60 million) is Western Europe's largest country. Its art, architecture, music and literature are famous. Farming is important, but France is also a great industrial power.

French is the world's third most widely spoken language, after English and Chinese. But France itself has several minority languages, including Breton in the north-west, Basque and Catalan in the south, German in the north-east, and

▲The average age for marriage in England and Wales is just over 25 for men and 23 for women. The clothes worn at many weddings reflect the strong sense of tradition in British society.

◀Seen from the top of the Eiffel Tower in Paris, France, the traffic looks like toys. The grey structure at the bottom of the picture is the base of the Eiffel Tower itself.

Vineyards grow in many European countries. France is the leading producer of quality wine. Italy, Spain, the USSR and West Germany are other major producers.

The gently sloping vineyards of the Bordeaux wine-growing area of France (**above**), contrast with the steep hillsides of Germany's Rhine wine region (**right**).

Provençal in the south-east.

Two tiny countries lie on France's borders. Monaco (population 26,000) is on the south-east, on the Mediterranean coast. Andorra (32,000) is in the Pyrenees mountains, between France and Spain.

Germany was split into two nations in 1945, after its defeat in World War 2. West Germany (61.7 million) is allied to the West, while East Germany is a Communist country. West Germany was in ruins in 1945. But, through hard work the Germans recovered quickly. West Germany is now Western Europe's leading industrial nation.

The mountainous Alpine region of south-central Europe includes Austria (population 7.5 million), Switzerland (6.5 million) and tiny Liechtenstein (26,000). Switzerland has three official languages: German, French and Italian. Another language, called Romansch, is spoken by a few people in the south-east. The Swiss are skilled craftsmen. Their clocks and precision instruments are famous. Switzerland is a neutral country and is a centre for many banks and international organizations. These activities have made Switzerland wealthy. Austria is also prosperous. Like Switzerland, it attracts tourists who enjoy winter sports and mountain scenery.

SOUTHERN EUROPE

Southern Europe is generally poorer than the north. Many village traditions survive. For example, the husband is usually regarded as the protector of the family and his wife occupies a secondary role.

Spain (population 40 million) is the largest European country apart from France. It shares the Iberian peninsula with Portugal (9.8 million) and a British colony, Gibraltar (30,000). Spain claims Gibraltar, but the people of Gibraltar want to stay British. Spain has four major languages. The official language is Spanish (or Castilian). Galician is spoken in the north-west, Basque in the north-centre and Catalan in the north-east. These language groups have been given local governments with limited powers. But some Basques, whose language is not related to any other, favour independence from Spain.

Spain was a poor country 50 years ago, but it has made much progress in recent years. It is now wealthier than Portugal, which, like Spain, once ruled a large empire.

Italy (population 56.2 million) was the centre of Roman civilization. It is known for its art, sculpture and opera. It is fairly prosperous, but the south is poor by comparison with the industrialized north. Italy's capital, Rome, contains the tiny independent nation called Vatican City (population 1,000). It contains the government of the Roman Catholic Church. Another small territory enclosed within Italy is San Marino (21,000).

The sunny climate of Malta (364,000), an island nation south of Italy, attracts tourists, as do the islands of Greece in south-eastern Europe. Greece (9.7 million) has many fascinating ancient ruins. But today it is one of Europe's less developed nations.

▲This Albanian village is in the mountainous interior. Albania, in south-eastern Europe, is one of the continent's poorest countries. More than 60 per cent of Albanians work on farms.

EASTERN EUROPE

Eastern Europe has mainly lagged behind the west in its economic development. This is partly because it has less resources and partly because of the more severe climate, especially its long, cold winters.

The term 'Eastern Europe' is often used for the eight Communist nations in Europe. Six of them are allied to the USSR: Poland (population 35.9 million), Romania (22.5 million), East Germany (16.7 million), Czechoslovakia (15.3 million), Hungary (10.7 million) and Bulgaria (8.9 million). Two other countries have independent Communist governments: Yugoslavia (22.5 million) and Albania (2.8 million).

Farming was once the main activity in eastern Europe. But in the last 40 years, many industries have been created with help from the USSR and China (in the case of Albania). This is especially true of East Germany and Poland, which are now major industrial powers. All industries are government-owned. In most of the countries, there are two kinds of farms: government-owned farms on which workers are paid wages; and large collective farms run by a group of families who share the produce. However, the Poles opposed this policy and the government was forced to give in. Today, about three-quarters of Poland's farmland is privately owned.

▲The Parthenon is an ancient Greek temple in Athens, Greece. It recalls the glories of ancient Greece, a civilization which helped to shape western societies.

► Women work with men on farms in Bulgaria. In 1980, 37 out of every 100 workers were employed on farms, as compared with 39 in industry.

▲ Many of the Eastern European Communist countries lack modern equipment that people in western countries take for granted. This method of weighing grapes in an Hungarian vineyard is very old-fashioned.

Poland is unusual in other ways. Communist governments discourage religious worship. One country, Albania, has closed its Muslim mosques and Christian churches. But about four out of every five Poles regularly attend Roman Catholic masses. In recent years, the Poles have asked for more freedom, including free *trade unions*. Polish workers set up an association of free trade unions, called Solidarity, but it was banned in 1981. Discontent with Communism has also been expressed in Czechoslovakia and Hungary.

About three-fifths of East Europeans are Slavs, who speak Balto-Slavic languages. Non-Slavs include Albanians, Germans, Hungarians and Romanians, together with smaller groups of Gypsies, Jews and Turks.

THE USSR

The Union of Soviet Socialist Republics (USSR) is also called the Soviet Union. In area it is the world's largest nation, with 268 million people. The country is divided into 15 Republics. The largest is the Russian Soviet Federal Socialist Republic, which covers 76 per cent of the USSR.

One-quarter of the USSR is in Europe and the rest is in Asia. The Russian language is one of about 60 spoken in the USSR. The largest group of people are Slavs, including Russians (52 per cent) and Ukrainians (16 per cent). About 75 per cent of the people live in the European part of the USSR.

The USSR has been a Communist country since 1917. Communism aims at stopping people being too rich or too poor. As a result, the Communist government stopped all private ownership, although the methods it used were often cruel. The aim of the Communists was to make the USSR a great industrial and military power. They have succeeded. At the end of World War 2 the USSR and the USA emerged as the two superpowers. The USSR's power is backed by huge natural resources and advanced technology.

▲This farm is in Kazakhstan in the Asian USSR. It is a collective farm, or kolkhoz. Here, the farmers work together and share the produce. Each family on a collective farm also has its own small plot of land.

▼Samarkand is a city in Uzbekistan, in the Asian USSR. It contains the tomb of Tamerlane (1336–1405), the Mongol ruler of Samarkand. Tamerlane was a great soldier and conquered much of south-western Asia and northern India.

Life has changed for people in the USSR. In 1913, 75 per cent of the workforce was employed on farms. Poverty was common. By 1980, farming employed 14 per cent of the workforce, industry 45 per cent and services (the service industries are those, as the name suggests, that provide a service, such as transport or hairdressing) 41 per cent. (For comparison, in the USA the figures are 2 per cent, 32 per cent and 66 per cent.) Most people have comfortable lives. They get free health services and rents average only about 3 per cent of a worker's family income. But people must not criticise the Communist system. People who do so, called dissidents, are harshly treated. The law also forbids religious education for children under 18. Yet many millions of the people attend Russian Orthodox, Armenian Orthodox, Georgian Orthodox, Roman Catholic and Protestant churches, while millions more follow Islam and Judaism.

5 THE PEOPLE OF ASIA

▼Relief map of Asia, south-east Asia, the Indian sub-continent, and south-west Asia or the Middle East.

Asia, the largest continent, is made up of 39 independent nations, together with 75 per cent of the USSR and 97 per cent of Turkey. Asia contains about three-fifths of the world's population.

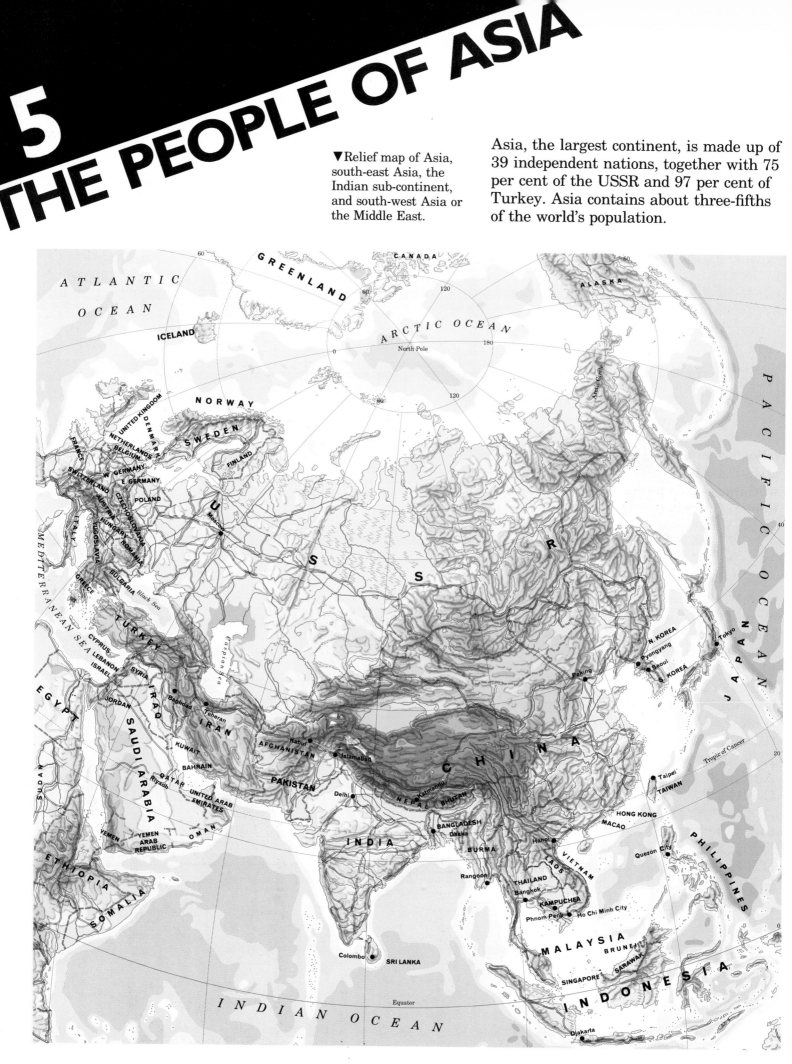

CIVILIZATIONS AND RELIGIONS

Around 5,000 years ago, early civilizations, starting with the Sumerian, grew up in south-western Asia in the valleys of the Tigris and Euphrates rivers. About 4,500 years ago, another major civilization developed in the Indus river valley and spread into northern India. Other civilizations developed in northern and central China from about 3,500 years ago.

Besides being the 'cradle of civilization', Asia was also the birthplace of the world's major religions: Hinduism, Buddhism, Shintoism, Judaism, Taoism, Confucianism, Christianity and Islam. Asia's religions have spread widely. The religion with the greatest number of followers is Christianity. There are now about 1,070 million Christians in the world, about 73 per cent of whom are Roman Catholics.

PEOPLE AND LANGUAGES

Caucasoid people live in south-western and southern Asia from Turkey to Bangladesh. They include Arabs, Jews, *Irano-Afghans* and most people in India. But the Veddoid people of southern India and Sri Lanka are descendants of an earlier people (page 10).

Mongoloid people include the so-called Classic Mongoloids. This group includes Eskimos, the Japanese (but not the Ainu), the Koreans and the northern Chinese. The southern Chinese, who are shorter, sturdier people, belong to the Indonesian-Malay group, together with Burmese, Filipinos, Thais and many others. Other major groups in Asia include the Turkic peoples of central Asia and the Tibetans.

▶The people of Asia include Irano-Afghans (1) and Arabs (2) in south-western Asia; Russians (3) some of whom are Caucasoids and some Mongoloids; the Mongoloid Indonesian-Malays (4); Indians (5), Chinese (6) and Siberians (7), who belong to the Mongoloid sub-group of the human family.

The languages of Asia are grouped into several language families. The Indo-European family includes Bengali and Hindustani in India and the Iranian languages of Persian and Pashto. Semitic languages, including Arabic and Hebrew, are also spoken in south-western Asia. Dravidian languages, for example Tamil, Telugu and Malayalam, are spoken in southern India and Sri Lanka. The Uralic and Altaic language families include Turkish, Manchu and Mongol. The Sino-Tibetan group includes Chinese, Burmese, Thai and Tibetan. And Japanese and Korean together form a language family of their own.

NORTH-EASTERN ASIA

on the island of Taiwan. About four-fifths of the people in Communist China live in rural (country) areas. Most live in groups of villages, called communes. Here, everyone works together and shares the products of the commune.

China is a developing country, but it is changing quickly. It is an important world power, and now follows policies independently of the other major communist power, the USSR. At home, it has made great advances in farming, mining and manufacturing. It has raised the living standards of the peasants. And the fact that women work alongside men in the communes has made them equal with men. But problems remain. The population is increasing by about 14 million a year. The government is trying

▲Chopsticks are used at a family party. In the past, most Chinese people lived close to their relations in extended family groups. On holidays, sometimes as many as 200 members of an extended family would gather together. The extended family has declined since 1949, when China became a Communist country.

North-eastern Asia includes three Communist countries: China (population 1,008 million), North Korea (18.7 million) and Mongolia (1.7 million), an ally of the USSR. The non-Communist countries are Japan (118.4 million), South Korea (39.3 million) and Taiwan (18.7 million). There are also two small territories on China's south coast. They are Hong Kong, a British colony, and Macao, ruled by Portugal.

China has more people than any other country. About 94 per cent are Han, or true Chinese. But there are also large minorities, including Manchus, Mongols, Tibetans and Uighurs. China became a Communist country in 1949. The anti-Communists founded a separate country

▲This Japanese couple wear a mixture of western and eastern clothes on their wedding day. But despite western influences, most couples follow ancient Shinto traditions in the wedding ceremonies.

►The Ainu are descendants of the first inhabitants of Japan. Some still live on Hokkaido island. The Ainu are a non-Mongoloid, or 'Archaic white', people.

◄Mongolia consists largely of a windswept plateau. The people once led wandering lives. But the Communist government has reorganized farming. Many people have been resettled on collective farms, like those in the USSR.

to persuade people to marry later and have small families.

The other world power in north-eastern Asia is Japan, Asia's only truly industrialized country. Western influences can be seen, but old traditions are strong. The Japanese have always regarded themselves less as individuals and more as members of a group, such as a family or the nation. As a result, Japanese workers are loyal to the company for which they work. In turn, the company helps the workers, increasing their pay when they have children and giving them bonuses when the company makes a profit. Because of the group spirit in companies, most Japanese stay with the same company throughout their working lives. This stability in industry has helped to make Japan one of the world's richest nations.

Israel was founded in 1948 as a Jewish nation. But local Palestinians opposed the creation of Israel. They were supported by Arab nations who fought wars with Israel in 1948, 1956, 1967 and 1973. But the Israelis have worked hard. They have turned deserts into farmland and have built up mining and manufacturing industries.

The Arab countries were once extremely poor. But several have become wealthy because of their oil deposits. Leading oil producers include Iran (population 41.2 million), Iraq (14.2 million), Saudi Arabia (10 million), Syria (9.5 million), Kuwait (1.6 million), the United Arab Emirates (1.1 million), Oman (919,000), Bahrain (362,000) and

▼In spite of the great wealth that oil has brought to many of the countries of south-west Asia, many peoples throughout the region still follow the traditional ways of life. These Iranian nomads, with their big dark tents, travel from place to place as their ancestors have done for many centuries.

SOUTH-WESTERN ASIA

South-western Asia is sometimes called the Middle or Near East. It contains 17 nations. All, except Israel (population 4 million) and Cyprus (623,000), are Muslim countries, although both of these countries have sizeable Muslim minorities. And all except Afghanistan, Cyprus, Iran, Israel and Turkey are Arab countries and use Arabic as their chief language.

Qatar (236,000). Money from oil sales has been widely used to modernize the countries. But other Arab countries, including the Yemen Arab Republic (7.2 million), Jordan (3.4 million) and South Yemen (2 million) are still poor.

South-western Asia faces many problems. Lebanon (2.7 million) has suffered civil wars between Arab Christians and Muslims. And the Kurds, a minority in Turkey (46.5 million), the USSR, Iran, Iraq and Syria want to create their own country. In the 1960s they were defeated by Iraqi troops.

Iran and Iraq began a long war in 1980 and Soviet troops have been in Afghanistan (population 16.8 million) since 1979. They claim they are helping the pro-USSR Afghan government to put down Muslim rebels.

SOUTHERN ASIA

Southern Asia includes India (population 717 million), Bangladesh (93 million) and Pakistan (87 million). These countries once formed British India. When British India became independent in 1947 it was divided into two countries: India which was mainly Hindu, and Pakistan which was principally Muslim. Pakistan had two provinces: West and East Pakistan. In 1971 East Pakistan broke away and became Bangladesh. The other south Asian countries are Sri Lanka (formerly Ceylon population 15.2 million), and two mountain kingdoms: Nepal (15.4 million) and Bhutan (1.2 million).

Southern Asia is extremely poor. People there live, on average, for a much shorter time than people in Western nations. On average, people live to the ages of 43 in Bhutan, 46 in Nepal, 48 in Bangladesh, 50 in Pakistan, 55 in India and 69 in Sri Lanka. Compare these with average life expectancies of 74 in Britain and 75 in the USA.

The people suffer because of divisions caused by different languages, religions and political views. India is especially complex. Its population is increasing by nearly 16 million a year. This puts a great strain on India's limited resources. India has 15 major national languages

▲An Afghan herdsman looks after his livestock. Many Afghans take their animals to graze on the high mountain pastures in summer, just like the farmers in central Europe. The farmers return to sheltered valleys in winter.

▼This woman in Nepal is a Sherpa. Sherpa women work hard on farms and make textiles and colourful clothes. Their husbands, who are famed as guides and mountaineers, do not dominate them.

and hundreds of other minor languages and *dialects*. Some 82.7 per cent of the people are Hindus. There are also Muslims (11.2 per cent), Christians (2.6 per cent), Sikhs (1.9 per cent) and Buddhists (0.7 per cent). Religious and other differences cause unrest, and make it difficult for the government to keep the country united.

SOUTH-EASTERN ASIA

South-eastern Asia consists of 10 nations: Thailand (population 48.5 million), Burma (34.9 million), Malaysia (14.5 million), Singapore (2.5 million) and three Communist nations: Kampuchea (Cambodia) (7.1 million), Vietnam (5.7 million) and Laos (3.5 million). There are two island nations: Indonesia (152.6 million) and the Philippines (50.7 million). Brunei (233,000), a small, oil-rich nation on the island of Borneo, became independent of Britain in 1983.

Most of this tropical, largely forested region is under-developed, and the majority of people are poor farmers. The only industrialized country is the small nation of Singapore, which has an energetic Chinese community. Malaysia has some resources and is the second most developed country in the region.

South-eastern Asia contains a great variety of peoples and languages. Buddhism is a major religion. Islam is important in Malaysia and Singapore. The Philippines is the only Asian country with a Christian (mainly Roman Catholic) majority.

◄This Indian couple wears elaborate head coverings for their marriage ceremony. The coverings mark the solemnity of the occasion.

◄These young dancers live on the island of Bali, in Indonesia. Bali's music, dance and drama is used mainly to tell ancient Hindu legends, although the leading religion in most of Indonesia is Islam.

▲Many Asian farmers take crops which are not needed for their families to the cities. There, they sell the produce in markets. This 'floating market' is in Bangkok, capital of Thailand, in south-eastern Asia.

6 THE PEOPLE OF AFRICA

▶Relief map of the African continent.

Africa, the second largest continent, contains 51 independent nations; six of them are island nations.

AFRICAN CIVILIZATIONS

North-eastern Africa was the home, about 5,000 years ago, of the great civilization of ancient Egypt. North Africa was important in the ancient world. Africa south of the Sahara had its own cultures, but none as brilliant as ancient Egypt.

Until the nineteenth century, Europeans knew little of Africa south of the Sahara. In the late nineteenth century, Africa was shared out between Belgium, Britain, France, Germany, Portugal and Spain. By 1914, only Ethiopia and Liberia were free from foreign rule. The Europeans introduced Christianity and a *money* economy.

After World War 2 African countries began to win their independence. By 1984, the only country on the African mainland which was not independent was Namibia (population 1 million). It was ruled by South Africa.

The cultures of modern Africa are based mainly on European and African traditions. But the continent is poor and the different countries find national unity hard to achieve, partly because there are more than 1,000 languages in Africa. Because they are unstable, many countries have military governments.

PEOPLES, LANGUAGES AND RELIGIONS

Berbers were the original people of North Africa when the Arabs conquered the area in the seventh century AD. Both Berbers and Arabs are Caucasoids. Other Caucasoids include Egyptians, many Sudanese, Ethiopians and Somalis. But the Ethiopians and Somalis have mixed with Negroid peoples.

Negroid, or Black, people live south of the Sahara. West African Blacks live between Senegal and Nigeria. They speak Niger-Congo and Sudanic languages. Blacks speaking languages belonging to the Bantu family live south of a line drawn across Africa from Cameroon to Kenya. Another Negroid group, the Nilotes, live in the region drained by the White Nile river. Many Nilotes are tall, as are many Nilo-Hamites, including the Masai of Kenya and Tanzania. Nilo-Hamites are a mixture of Nilotes and Caucasoid people.

Pygmies are hunter-gathers, who were the first people of central Africa. They grow to 137–142 cm (4ft 6in–4ft 8in) in height and have a dark brown skin. The first people in southern Africa belonged to the Khoisan group. They are better

▼The map shows that Africa produces many crops and minerals. Many of their products are exported to countries in the western world. Most of Africa, except for South Africa and Egypt, have few manufacturing industries.

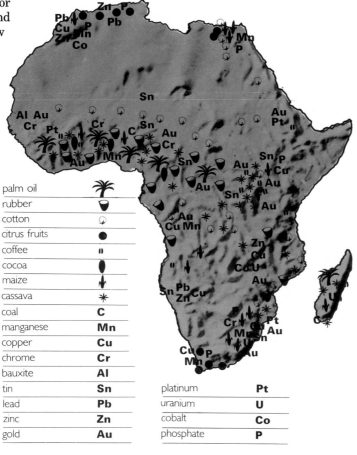

palm oil	🌴
rubber	🍷
cotton	☖
citrus fruits	●
coffee	‖
cocoa	◗
maize	↓
cassava	✳
coal	**C**
manganese	**Mn**
copper	**Cu**
chrome	**Cr**
bauxite	**Al**
tin	**Sn**
lead	**Pb**
zinc	**Zn**
gold	**Au**

platinum	**Pt**
uranium	**U**
cobalt	**Co**
phosphate	**P**

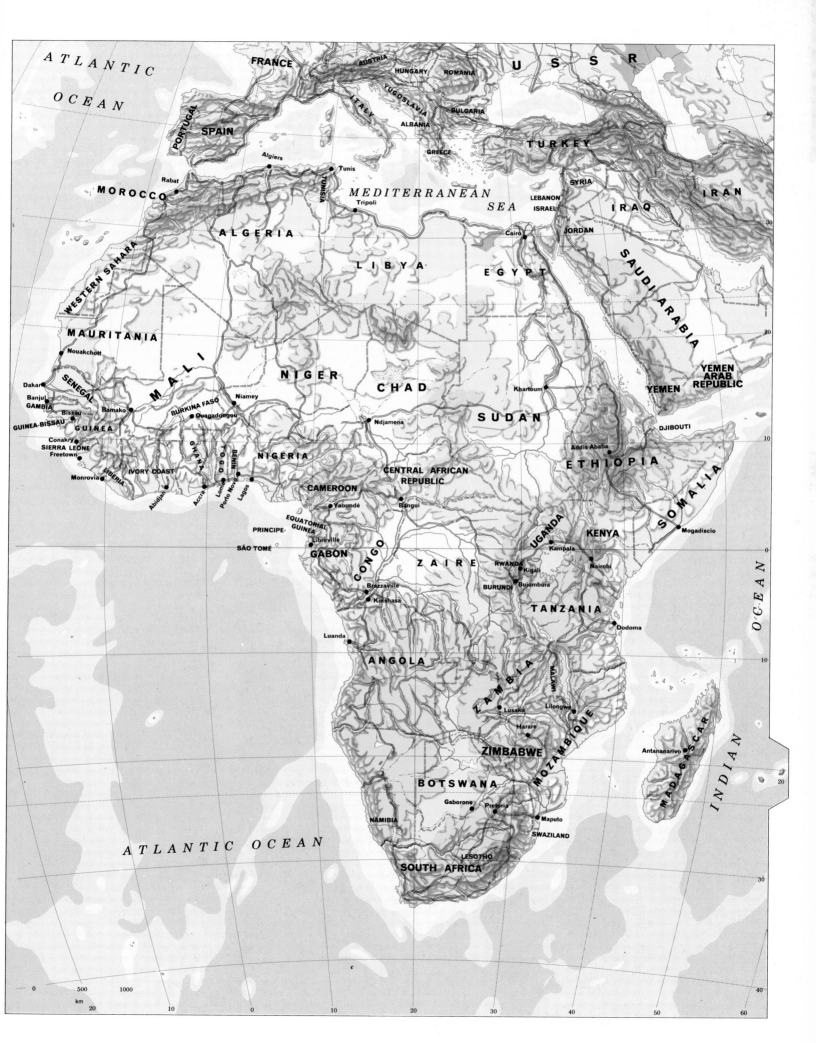

ATLANTIC

OCEAN

FRANCE

AUSTRIA

HUNGARY

ROMANIA

U S S R

ITALY

YUGOSLAVIA

BULGARIA

PORTUGAL

SPAIN

ALBANIA

GREECE

TURKEY

Algiers

Tunis

SYRIA

IRAN

Rabat

MEDITERRANEAN   SEA

LEBANON

IRAQ

MOROCCO

TUNISIA

Tripoli

ISRAEL

JORDAN

Cairo

WESTERN SAHARA

ALGERIA

LIBYA

EGYPT

SAUDI ARABIA

MAURITANIA

Nouakchott

M A L I

N I G E R

C H A D

Khartoum

YEMEN
ARAB
REPUBLIC

Dakar

SENEGAL

YEMEN

Banjul

Niamey

DJIBOUTI

GAMBIA

Bamako

BURKINA FASO

SUDAN

Bissau

Ouagadougou

Ndjamena

Addis Ababa

GUINEA-BISSAU

GUINEA

Conakry

GHANA

NIGERIA

ETHIOPIA

SOMALIA

SIERRA LEONE

Freetown

TOGO

BENIN

CENTRAL AFRICAN
REPUBLIC

Monrovia

LIBERIA

IVORY COAST

CAMEROON

Mogadiscio

Abidjan

Accra

Lome

Porto Novo

Lagos

Yaoundé

Bangui

UGANDA

KENYA

PRINCIPE

EQUATORIAL
GUINEA

Kampala

SÃO TOMÉ

Libreville

GABON

CONGO

ZAIRE

RWANDA

Kigali

Nairobi

BURUNDI

Bujumbura

Brazzaville

Kinshasa

TANZANIA

Luanda

Dodoma

ANGOLA

Z A M B I A

MALAWI

Lusaka

Lilongwe

Harare

ZIMBABWE

MOZAMBIQUE

Antananarivo

MADAGASCAR

INDIAN

BOTSWANA

OCEAN

Gaborone

Pretoria

NAMIBIA

Maputo

SWAZILAND

ATLANTIC   OCEAN

LESOTHO

SOUTH AFRICA

0   500   1000
km

41

The Arabs have crossed the Sahara desert in camel caravans since the early Middle Ages. Much of our knowledge of early Black empires comes from the accounts of Arab writers.

known as Bushmen and Hottentots. Bushmen are slightly taller than pygmies, and have yellowish-brown skin. Some are still hunter-gatherers in the Kalahari desert of south-western Africa. A few Hottentots survive in Namibia.

Islam is the religion of North Africa. Some Black Africans are Muslims, some are Christians and some follow traditional beliefs. The old religions often include the idea that there is only one God, although many people believe in *ancestor worship* and that spirits occupy every part of Nature.

Africa's people are unevenly distributed. Large areas, including the Sahara and some densely forested regions near the Equator, are thinly populated.

NORTHERN AFRICA

The northernmost countries of Africa, Egypt (population 44.3 million), Morocco (20.3 million), Algeria (19.9 million), Tunisia (6.7 million) and Libya (3.2 million) are among Africa's richer countries. Egypt has many industries, and Libya and Algeria produce much oil and natural gas.

The southern parts of these countries, together with Sudan (20.2 million), Mali (7.1 million), Niger (5.9 million), Chad (4.5 million) and northern Mauritania (1.6 million) are covered by the burning-hot Sahara. The people of the north are Arabs and Berbers. Their ways of life differ from those of the Black peoples in the south and these differences have caused civil wars in Chad and Sudan.

South of the Sahara is a dry grazing region called the Sahel. Here, overgrazing by livestock and the cutting down of trees for firewood has exposed the soil. During droughts, winds have blown away the

◄Africa's people include Caucasoid Arabs and Berbers, top left, and Black people in western and southern Africa, bottom left. Pygmies, centre top, and Bushmen, centre bottom, are descendants of early inhabitants of Africa. Nilo-Hamites include the Masai of eastern Africa, top right. Most people in southern Africa are Blacks, bottom right. They speak one of the many Bantu languages of central and southern Africa.

44

Farmers sell produce at a market in Morocco, in North Africa. People from other countries would not recognize some of the things on sale. This is because crops and diets vary around the world.

Fruits and other foods are on sale in this market in Mali, north-western Africa. The people here, in southern Mali, are Blacks, although in northern Mali the population is made up of Arab and Berber peoples.

loose soil and the land becomes desert. Millions of livestock have died and many people have starved.

WEST AFRICA

West Africa includes Nigeria (population 90.6 million), Ghana (12.2 million), Ivory Coast (8.9 million), Burkina Faso (formerly Upper Volta, 6.5 million), Senegal (6 million), Guinea (5.7 million), Benin (3.7 million), Sierra Leone (3.2 million), Togo (2.8 million), Liberia (2 million), Guinea-Bissau (790,000), Gambia (587,000) and the island nation of Cape Verde (300,000). Most West African countries are poor, although Nigeria has become fairly prosperous because of its oil reserves. And Ivory Coast has set up many manufacturing industries.

French, English and Portuguese are the official languages of these countries. African languages are not used, because there are too many of them. For instance, Nigeria has about 240 languages and dialects. None is spoken widely enough to be a national language and so English is used for official purposes.

São Tomé and Principe (115,000). Most people in these countries are poor farmers, many practising shifting cultivation (page 22). But Cameroon, Congo, Gabon and Zaire have minerals which they sell abroad (export).

This region is occupied mainly by Bantu-speaking peoples, with a few pygmies in the forests. Language and other differences have caused unrest, particularly in Zaire.

CENTRAL AFRICA

Central Africa has Zaire (population 30.7 million), Cameroon (9.3 million), the Central African Republic (2.4 million), Congo (1.7 million), Gabon (669,000), Equatorial Guinea (346,000) and the island nation of

EAST AFRICA

East Africa includes Ethiopia (population 32.9 million), Somalia (4.5 million) and Djibouti (381,000). These countries have been hard hit by the droughts which have struck the Sahel. Terrible famines have occurred. To the south lie Tanzania

▲Masai women wear huge necklaces and earrings. The Masai are of mixed Negroid and Caucasoid origin. They live in Kenya and Tanzania. Their traditional diet is a mixture of milk and cattle blood.

▼Music, especially drumming, singing and dancing are leading art forms in Black Africa. These dancers are Zulus, who live in South Africa. Many African dances have a religious meaning.

(19.8 million), Kenya (18.1 million), Uganda (14.5 million), Rwanda (5.5 million) and the small but thickly populated Burundi (4.3 million).

East Africa also has a great variety of people. In Ethiopia, the army has fought Eritreans, who live on the Red Sea coast, and Somali-speakers, who live in the south-east. Both of these groups would like to break away from Ethiopia. In Burundi, Rwanda and Uganda, there has also been much loss of life because of cultural differences. But Kenya, with about 40 language groups, and Tanzania, with 120, have been mostly stable.

SOUTHERN AFRICA

Southern Africa includes the island nations of Madagascar (population 9.2 million), Mauritius (971,000), Comoros (358,000) and the Seychelles (63,000). On the mainland are Mozambique (12.9 million) and Angola (3.1 million) which were once Portuguese colonies. South Africa (30.4 million), Zimbabwe (7.5 million), Malawi (6.5 million), Zambia (6.0 million), Lesotho (1.4 million), Botswana (930,000) and Swaziland (641,000) were formerly British.

South Africa is Africa's most developed country. It has the largest and best-equipped armed forces. But it faces many problems. Its people are divided into four main groups. People of European origin make up 17.5 per cent of the total, Blacks 70.2 per cent, Coloureds (of mixed origin) 9.4 per cent, and people of Asian descent 2.9 per cent.

Since South Africa became independent in 1910, the government and the country's great wealth have been controlled by the European minority. Under the policy of *apartheid* the Blacks have been granted 10 Homelands, or Bantustans, about 13 per cent of the country. There, they can elect their own governments. But they have no rights in the rest of the country, where more than half of them must live and work. Most countries have criticised South Africa, arguing that it is practising *racial discrimination*.

A Bushman making
fire with two sticks and
some dry grass. In
skilled hands this is
quite an efficient way
of making fire.

47

7 THE PEOPLE OF OCEANIA

Oceania consists of Australia (population 15.2 million), New Zealand (3.2 million), Papua New Guinea (3.1 million), and many islands scattered across the Pacific Ocean.

The first people in Australia were Australoids called Tasmanian Aborigines. They were driven south into the island of Tasmania when the ancestors of the modern Australian Aborigines arrived by sea from Asia about 16,000 years ago.

The Europeans treated the Tasmanian Aborigines so badly that they died out in 1876. The Australian Aborigines are called 'archaic Whites', because anthropologists think they are Caucasoid (White), but of an ancient type.

The Pacific islanders are divided into three groups. The Polynesians, including New Zealand's Maoris, are believed to be a mixture of archaic Whites and Mongoloids. The Micronesians in the northern Pacific are similar to the Polynesians. The third group consists of dark-skinned Melanesians, including Papuans and small Negrito people.

▼Relief map showing Oceania and the coastal fringes of the surrounding continents.

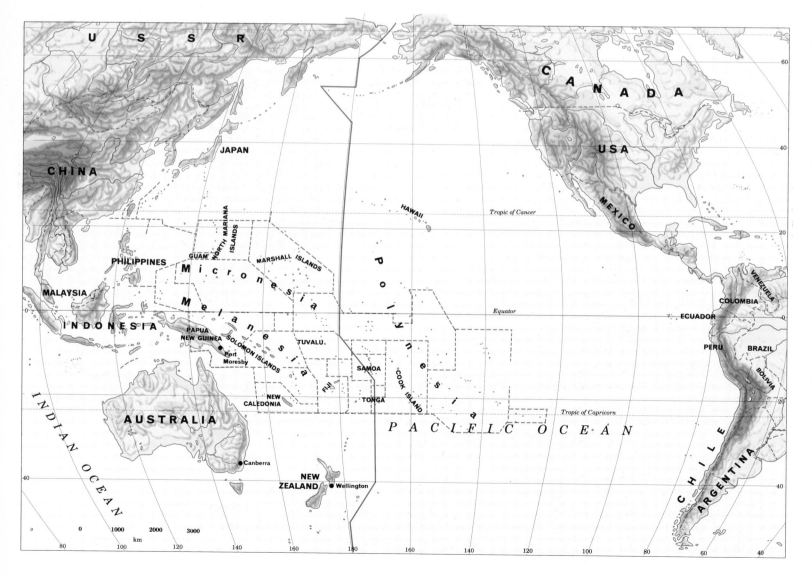

AUSTRALIA AND NEW ZEALAND

Most Australians are of European, especially British, descent. But since World War 2 many immigrants have arrived from Italy, Greece, the Netherlands, Germany and other European countries. Australia also has tiny Chinese, Indian and Japanese minorities, together with about 136,000 Aborigines (including people of mixed Aborigine and European descent). The Aborigines were once neglected and lived in great poverty. Today, they are helped in many ways. Reservations have been set aside for those who want to continue their traditional way of life as hunters.

The first settlers, convicts, were landed in Australia in 1788 and the first free settlers arrived from Britain in 1793. Australia offered many opportunities for energetic people. The country is now prosperous and highly industrialized. About 89 per cent of the people live in cities and towns. Since 1973, when Britain joined the European Economic Community, Australia's ties with Britain have weakened. British traditions remain strong, however, and the British Queen is still Queen of Australia. But many Australians see their country as a Pacific Ocean power rather than as an ally of

▲Australian Aborigines use spears to hunt. They hurl the spears from special spear throwers to give greater power to the throw and to make the spear go farther.

Britain.

New Zealand also has a British character. But like Australia, it also has settlers from other parts of Europe. New Zealand also became wealthy because of farming, especially sheep-rearing, although today, 85 per cent of the people live in cities and towns.

According to tradition, the Maoris settled in the country 650 years ago. They mixed with a similar Polynesian people they found there. In 1814, the Maoris probably numbered 100,000.

▲Aborigines prepare for a ritual ceremony by painting their bodies with complicated traditional patterns.

◄Sydney, in New South Wales, is Australia's largest city and a major port. The building on the left, which resembles a pile of seashells, is the Opera House.

►Maoris live in New Zealand. After many years of neglect, there is now a revival of interest in the culture of these Polynesian people.

Many died in wars with the British. By 1869, only about 42,000 were left, but they now number about 280,000. Many live and work in cities, meeting together in their leisure time in sporting clubs and other organizations.

PAPUA NEW GUINEA

Australia ruled Papua New Guinea, the eastern part of the island of New Guinea, until 1975. Most of the people are Melanesians. There are also some pygmy Negritos. Some people still follow their ancient tribal lifestyles. They fish, grow yams and sweet potatoes and rear pigs. Men and women once lived separately. The men's houses were used to plan raids on other tribes and battles and head-hunting were once common. More peaceful activities included feasting and dancing.

Many people have moved into the coastal towns and adopted western lifestyles. The towns have schools, which are mostly lacking in the interior.

PACIFIC ISLANDS

Besides Papua New Guinea, Melanesia also includes Fiji (population 646,000), the independent Solomon Islands (241,000), and Vanuatu (121,000). The French Overseas Territory of New Caledonia (143,000) is also Melanesian. The term Melanesia means 'islands of black people'. But the islands' populations now contain groups of Europeans, Chinese, Micronesians and Polynesians.

Polynesia means 'many islands'. It consists of the islands within a triangle formed by New Zealand, Easter Island and Hawaii, a state of the USA. Other island groups include Western Samoa (157,000), French Polynesia (150,000), Tonga (98,000), American Samoa (33,000), a New Zealand Territory, Cook Island (18,000), and Tuvalu (8,000).

Not all scholars agree on the origins of the Polynesians. Most think that they came from Asia, although some have suggested that they came from South America. The Polynesians are certainly superb sailors. Long before Europeans arrived, they navigated accurately on long sea journeys. They had an elaborate culture and complex religious beliefs. But these declined when Europeans arrived.

Micronesia means 'little islands'. There are more than 2,000 between the Philippines and Hawaii. They form Micronesia. They include Guam (110,000), the Marshall Islands (91,000), the Federated States of Micronesia (74,000), Kiribati (60,000), the North Mariana Islands (17,000) and the Republic of Belau (12,000).

▲ Once fierce and war-like, the tribesmen of Papua New Guinea now put on their superb headdresses and ornaments to impress tourists. Even so, they are awe-inspiring figures.

No humans permanently inhabit the icy wastes of Antarctica, only scientists stay for brief periods.

53

ANTARCTICA

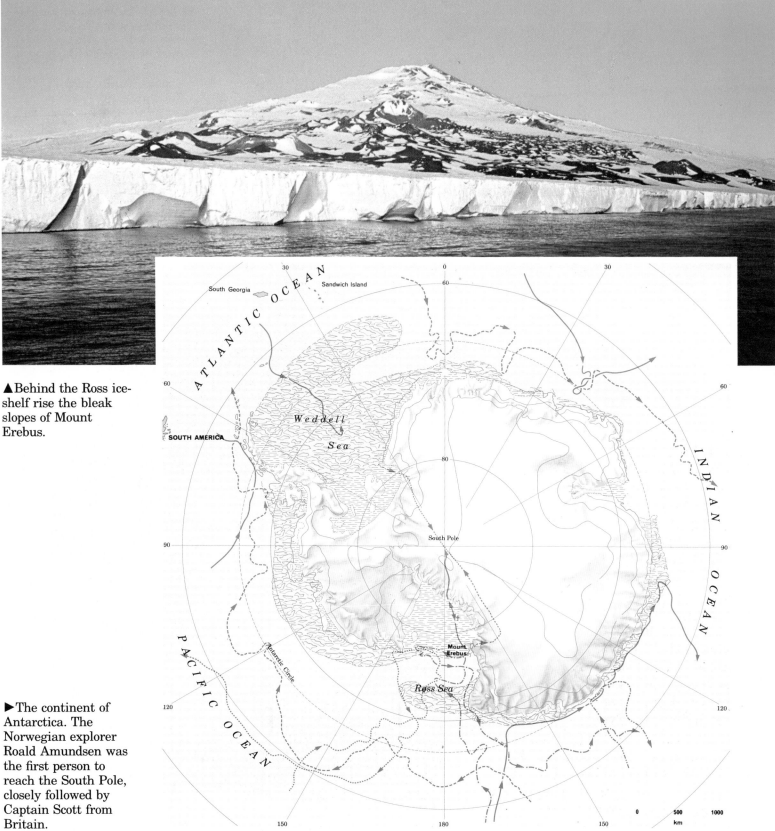

▲Behind the Ross ice-shelf rise the bleak slopes of Mount Erebus.

►The continent of Antarctica. The Norwegian explorer Roald Amundsen was the first person to reach the South Pole, closely followed by Captain Scott from Britain.

The continent of Antarctica, around the South Pole, is larger than either Europe or Oceania. But it has no permanent population. Most of Antarctica is hidden by a vast, thick ice sheet and is bitterly cold. The only people who go to Antarctica are fishermen and scientists. The scientists study such things as the weather and mineral resources. They live in heated homes, but must get all their supplies, including food and heating materials, from outside sources.

THE ARCTIC

◀Map of the Arctic Ocean. The American Lt-Commander Robert Peary was the first to reach the North Pole in 1909. Lt-Commander Richard Byrd, another American, was the first to fly over the North Pole in 1926. The Norwegian Roald Amundsen was the first to sail around North America through the Arctic Ocean in 1903–06.

The North Pole lies in the middle of the frozen Arctic Ocean. Around this ocean are Europe, Asia and North America. The northern parts of these continents lie within a region called the Arctic.

Several groups of people live in the cold and treeless Arctic, which is also called the *tundra*. The Lapps, who call themselves Samer, live in northern Europe. Some of these Caucasoid people are nomads, who follow the annual migrations of the reindeer (page 28). Most Lapps are short and stocky people.

The Arctic lands of northern Asia contain several groups of Mongoloid people, including the Evenki (or Tungus), Yakuts and Chukchees. These people also herd reindeer and hunt animals in the tundra and the forests to the south. The Chukchees live close to the Bering Strait. This was the crossing point for the ancestors of the North American Eskimos around 12,000 years ago. The North American Eskimos, called Inuits in Canada, traditionally lived by hunting, while children gathered berries during the short summer when plants bloom. The hunters once used harpoons and

spears, but firearms are now common. In winter, Eskimos lived in homes made of driftwood covered by soil, or in snow houses called igloos. In summer, they used tents. Many Eskimos have now adopted western lifestyles and live in modern homes.

▲The Eskimos were the only people who could live in the northernmost lands around the Arctic Ocean. Many have now given up their hard, traditional way of life.

9 OUR CHANGING WORLD

▼Skyscrapers like these in the USA are now seen in many cities throughout the world. High buildings can house a large number of people on a small area of land.

About 5 million people lived on Earth in 10,000 BC. After the invention of farming in about 8000 BC, the food supply increased and so did the number of people. By AD 1, about 200 million people were scattered around the world. By AD 1000, the total had reached 300 million. The rate of increase then began to speed up, with larger and larger annual increases. The 1,000 million mark was passed in the nineteenth century, the 2,000 million mark in the 1920s, and the 4,000 million mark in 1975.

THE PRESENT SITUATION

By the mid-1980s, our planet had about 4,800 million people. This means that, on average, about 32 people live on every square kilometre (83 per square mile). But vast areas, such as Antarctica, are empty. Other huge areas contain only a few bands of hunters. By contrast, some places are overpopulated. Overpopulation means that the land cannot support the people who live on it. People may survive when harvests are good. But when droughts occur and crops are ruined, then the people starve. The only way to prevent disaster is to supply food from other regions.

FUTURE POPULATION TRENDS

In the mid-1980s, the world's population was increasing by more than 80 million a year. Demographers (people who study population) predict that the world's population will continue to increase. But the rates of increase are slowing down in many industrialized countries. By contrast, the rates of increase are still rising in many of the world's poorest countries (though not in China or India). This means that the low living standards in many poor countries may become even lower as their populations increase. However, there are signs that as standards of living improve in these countries, the world's population will level out by the year 2100. But by then, the world will contain 10,200 million people.

The increase in population is having many effects on human society. Farmers are having to produce much more food every year. The Earth's energy and mineral resources are being used up at faster and faster rates every year. Manufacturing industries are increasing in number and size, and more and more people are living in crowded cities. And the space left for the plants and animals

►Pronghorns are North American animals. They were hunted almost to extinction in the 19th century. Now they are protected and their numbers have again increased.

which make our Earth such a beautiful place is growing smaller as cities and farms take up more and more land.

HARMING OUR EARTH

The effects of a fast-increasing population were seen in the USA in the nineteenth century. Farmers in the east cut down forests and farmers in the central plains ploughed up the grasslands. At first, they had rich harvests. But eventually, the soil's fertility declined and crop yields fell. In hilly areas in the east, the rain washed away grains of soil into the rivers. In the drier plains, the winds lifted up the powdery soil grains and carried them away. These are examples of *soil erosion.*

The farmers also greatly reduced the wildlife. The destruction of forests killed off forest animals. And such animals as the American antelope, or pronghorn, and the buffalo, or American bison, were hunted almost to extinction. A few survived and so we can still see these beautiful creatures. But many animals in other parts of the world have gone forever.

American scientists have studied soil erosion and they have found ways of controlling it. But their lessons are ignored in some places. For example, an estimated 202,000 square kilometres (78,000 square miles) of the Earth is, at present being turned into desert every year. It is caused by bad farming and droughts, as in Africa's Sahel region (page 44). And the world's rain forests are

▲Sadly, the needs of humans and animals often come into conflict. In Africa, when rivers are dammed to provide much-needed water for people and their crops, many hundreds of acres of bush are flooded, threatening the wildlife. This rhino has been tranquilized so that it can be taken to a game reserve and safety.

◄ Smoke and gases from power stations and factories pollute the air. Air pollution is a serious problem, especially in industrialized countries.

▶ This picture was taken in the 1930s in the Tennessee Valley in the eastern USA. It shows the results of bad farming methods. Today, soil erosion has been controlled in this region.

being cut down at a rate of 75,100 square kilometres (29,000 square miles) a year. Plants which have never been studied are vanishing completely. These plants might have provided us with valuable medicines, as other plants have done.

An increase in population also means an increase in industry and pollution. There are three kinds of pollution: air pollution, water pollution and land pollution. For example, factory smoke and gases from vehicle exhausts pollute the air. Factories also pollute water when they pump liquid wastes into rivers and coastal waters. And rubbish dumps, made up of industrial and domestic waste, are breeding grounds for flies and rats which spread disease.

The balance of nature
If we want to live in harmony with Nature, we must understand how it works. The study of how living things depend upon each other in a delicate 'balance of Nature' is the concern of scientists called ecologists. Ecology is a branch of *biology*. It is also concerned with the environments (surroundings) of living things and how they change.

For example, ecologists study food chains in various environments, from the primary producers (plants) to top animal predators which feed on other animals. The study of food chains helps us to understand what happens when we interfere with Nature. For example, pesticides are sprayed onto crops to kill insects. In this way, the harvest may be increased. But poisonous sprays may also

▼ Insect pests are killed with sprays. This raises crop yields. But the sprays may kill bacteria in the soil, making the land less fertile.

LOOKING AHEAD

kill bacteria in the soil. These bacteria help to keep the soil fertile. Birds absorb poison when they eat dead or dying insects and may die or be unable to produce eggs. Rain may wash poisonous pesticide into rivers and seas. There, fish absorb the poison. Sea birds which eat the fish are then poisoned. Even Arctic polar bears are not safe. Scientists have found large amounts of poisonous DDT in their bodies, because they ate poisoned fish. An understanding of how DDT has harmed Nature over vast areas has led many countries to ban its use.

The Earth is our home. If we spoil it by polluting or misusing it, we have nowhere else to go. Scientists are, therefore, seeking ways of controlling pollution. We must also protect the Earth and prevent unnecessary natural disasters, involving the extinction of animals. Ways must be found of conserving the Earth's resources, such as metals and fuels, as well as finding new ways of producing electrical energy. We must also protect the countryside and set up more national parks and reserves. Protected areas are not only havens for wildlife. They are also places where city dwellers can find peace in natural surroundings.

►Tsavo National Park, Kenya, is one of the world's largest areas set aside to protect wildlife. Such parks protect animal and plant life so that they can be enjoyed by future generations.

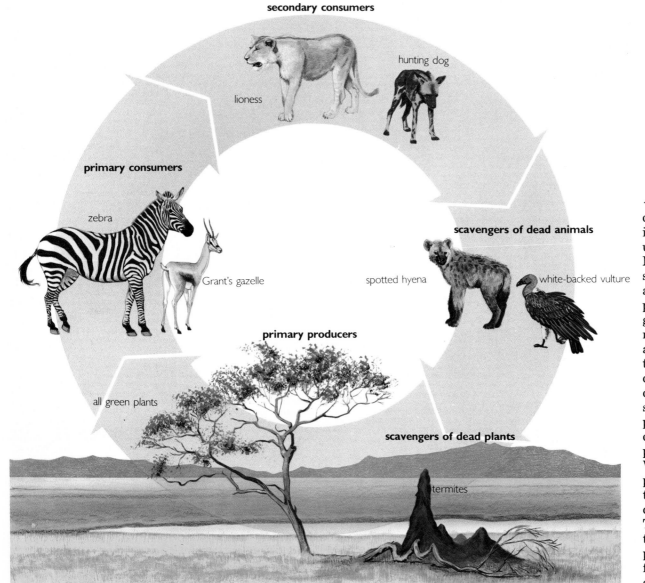

secondary consumers

lioness

hunting dog

primary consumers

zebra

Grant's gazelle

scavengers of dead animals

spotted hyena

white-backed vulture

primary producers

all green plants

scavengers of dead plants

termites

◄The study of food chains is of great importance in understanding how Nature works. The first stages in a food chain are the primary producers. These are green plants, which need sunlight, water and chemicals in order to grow. Animals, called primary consumers by scientists, eat the plants. Secondary consumers eat the primary consumers. When animals and plants die, bacteria in the soil break them down into chemicals. These chemicals are then absorbed by plants. In this way, food chains are continuous.

►Lapps live in the Arctic lands of northern Norway, Sweden, Finland and the USSR. Reindeer, which once supplied nearly all the food and clothing of the Lapps, are still kept in great herds for their meat and skins. This elderly couple enjoy the sunshine of the brief northern summer. The younger men will be away with the reindeer at the summer grazing grounds.

Adobe Sun-dried brick made from sandy clay or loam mixed with straw.

Agriculture Growing plants and rearing animals for food and other human needs.

Ancestor worship The belief that the souls of dead ancestors influence living people.

Anthropologist A person who studies people, their origins, languages, societies, and the like.

Apartheid A policy of keeping groups of a country's population segregated (separated) from one another.

Archaeologist A person who studies the ruins of old buildings and objects in order to find out how people lived in the past.

Australopithecus Scientific name meaning 'southern ape' given to a human-like creature that lived from about 4 million to 500,000 years ago. It walked upright. Scientists no longer believe it was an ancestor of humans.

Aztecs American Indians who founded a civilization in Mexico from the twelfth century AD.

Biology The study of living things. One division, botany, is concerned with plants. Zoology is concerned with animals.

Breeding Producing improved species of plants and animals.

Celtic languages A group of Indo-European languages, including Breton, Irish, Scots Gaelic and Welsh.

Census A count of the people of a country carried out by the government.

Colony A territory ruled by another country.

Communism/communist A political movement which aims at creating a classless society in which all property is held in common by the members of the society, not by individuals.

Confederacy An association of tribes, states or nations set up for a particular purpose.

Culture/cultural The sum total of the ways of life of a civilization or a group of people.

Developing country A poor country or one that has been only partly industrialized. Some wealthy countries, such as oil exporters, are still developing countries, because their economies as a whole are under-developed.

Dialect A variety of a language.

Epidemic A disease that attacks many people at one time. It may spread from place to place.

Extinct No longer existing.

Fossils Remains of ancient life preserved in rocks.

Government The system of ruling a country, or the group of persons who actually rule.

Homo erectus Scientific name meaning 'upright man' given to a more advanced human-like creature than *Australopithecus*. *Homo erectus* lived from about 1.6 million to 300,000 years ago.

Homo habilis Scientific name meaning 'handy man' given to a human-like creature that first appeared about 1.75 million years ago. Fossil remains show that *Homo habilis* made and used tools.

Homo sapiens The scientific name, meaning 'intelligent man', of modern human beings. This type of human first appeared about 500,000 years ago. Scientists subdivide the type. For example *Homo sapiens neanderthaliensis* lived between 100,000 and 10,000 years ago. Modern people, or *Homo sapiens sapiens*, appeared about 50,000 years ago.

Ice Ages Three periods in the Earth's history when ice sheets covered regions that are now warm. The most recent lasted from 2 million to 10 thousand years ago.

Industrial Revolution Period when factories and machines were widely used for the first time. In Britain this was the late eighteenth century.

Irano-Afghans Caucasoid people found mainly in Iran, Afghanistan and parts of Pakistan.

Irrigation channels Waterways dug by people to lead water to their fields.

Land reclamation Turning unproductive areas of land into farmland.

Mayas American Indians who founded civilizations in Central America between AD 350 and 1450.

Mestizos People of mixed Indian and European origin living in North America.

Migration The mass movement of animals or people.

Money economy A society where money is used to pay for goods and services; unlike bartering, which is the exchange of products or services for other products or services.

Mulattos People of mixed African and European descent.

Prehistoric Referring to a time before written historical records.

Primates Order of mammals, including humans, apes, monkeys and lemurs, that have nails rather than claws or hoofs.

Racial discrimination Prejudice, enmity or rivalry between groups of people because of their physical (racial) appearance and culture.

Ramapithecus A human-like ape that lived about 14 to 19 million years ago.

Soil erosion The rapid wearing away of the soil because of bad farming methods. Natural erosion is much slower.

Technology The application of science to practical uses.

Toltecs An American Indian people who founded a Central American civilization between AD 900 and 1200.

Trade unions Associations of workers that protect their common interests.

Tundra Region in the northern hemisphere too cold for trees to grow.

▼Drying is a very old method of preserving food. This Turkana woman from north-west Kenya is putting out fish to dry in the sun.

INDEX

Acknowledgments

Heather Angel, Australian News and Information Service, Anthony Blake, Ron Boardman, Camerapix Hutchison, Camera Press, J Allan Cash, N Cirani, Alan Clifton, G Dagli Orti, Explorer, EPS, Archivio IGDA, The Image Bank, International Colour Press, KLM Aerocarta, Roger Kohn, Marka, E Meunch, NASA, Novosti, Archivio P2, Picturepoint, Spectrum Colour Library, USDA, USIS, ZEFA.